Open Court Reading

Muse the Mule

A Division of The McGraw·Hill Companies

Columbus, Ohio

www.sra4kids.com

SRA/McGraw-Hill
A Division of The **McGraw·Hill** Companies

Copyright © 2002 by SRA/McGraw-Hill.

All rights reserved. Except as permitted under the United States Copyright Act, no part of this publication may be reproduced or distributed in any form or by any means, or stored in a database or retrieval system, without prior written permission from the publisher.

Printed in the United States of America.

Send all inquiries to:
SRA/McGraw-Hill
8787 Orion Place
Columbus, OH 43240-4027

ISBN 0-07-569735-1
3 4 5 6 7 8 9 DBH 05 04 03 02

Muse is a cute mule.
Muse lives in a forest
close to the Maze River.

Muse likes the forest and
the Maze River.
But Muse likes music the most.

Alfonso is a trader.
He cuts branches
and trades them at the river.
After Alfonso cuts big branches,
he puts them on Muse's back.

Muse does not like branches on his back.
Muse stands still and does not budge.

At last Alfonso plays music for Muse.
Alfonso plays nice music.

Muse does not like
big branches on his back.
But Muse likes Alfonso's music!